This journal belongs to:

____

Dedicated to my mother, the mother I am and all the mothers around who make this world a beautiful place in their own way. May this journal serve as a gentle reminder to nurture yourself as much as you nurture others.

As a mother, you juggle roles, and responsibilities, and often have little time for yourself. The Therapeutic Journal is here to offer you a much-needed me time to reconnect with yourself amidst the hustle of daily life. This is the first edition of The Therapeutic Journal and is specially designed for mothers. It aims to be your safe space to express your thoughts, process your feelings, and find clarity and purpose in your journey.

In the pages of this journal, you'll find guided prompts, mindfulness exercises, and reflective spaces designed to nurture your emotional well-being. Just 10 minutes to reflect, breathe, and reconnect with your inner self. With this journal, you can make that time truly yours, every day.

Let this journal be your personal retreat a place where each word you write brings you closer to the peace and balance you truly deserve. As a mother, you give so much of yourself to others. This journal is your time to give to you.

Dear Reader,

I am Priyanka Joshi, the founder of Sanity Daily and the creator of The Therapeutic Journal. As a single mother who does it all, I know firsthand what burnout feels like. I have learned to recognise the signs and understand when my body and mind are telling me it's time to slow down. It's this deep understanding of the overwhelming challenges mothers face that motivated me to create this journal.

My own journey with writing began during one of the most difficult times in my life recovering from an acute illness and navigating a challenging divorce while raising my beautiful daughter. Writing became my refuge, helping me process my emotions, find clarity, and ultimately a healing process.

As a mother, you give so much of yourself to everyone around you. This journal is your space to refill your cup. Some days, you might not feel like writing, and other days, you may pour your heart out. Both are okay. The Therapeutic Journal is born from a very personal experience. It's not just a journal of prompts; it's a powerful tool designed to help you reconnect with your inner self.

Whether you're looking to process emotions, manage stress, or simply find a moment of calm amidst the chaos of motherhood, this journal will guide you with grace and resilience. I created this journal for mothers like you who give their all, every single day, and sometimes forget to take a moment for themselves. You only need 10 minutes a day to embrace your Me Time, and with this journal, you'll find a safe space to reflect, breathe, and restore balance in your life.

I am honoured to share this journey with you and truly hope this journal brings you the same peace, clarity, and healing that writing has brought me.

Love & light,
Priyanka Joshi

In this JOURNAL

Getting Started

Before we get started, I would like to congratulate you and say thank you for picking up this journal in your self-help journey. To make it more effective and personal, I want to be your accountability coach throughout the period you use this journal and even after it, as you become a part of our big community.

I have left a few blank pages as your free writing space in the end for you to continue exploring your thoughts on paper. I have also added a weekly planner in between but please feel free to plan your journalling style your way and at the pace you feel comfortable with, remember there is no right or wrong way to do it.

Just enjoy this journey.

A Guided Journey into Journalling for Mothers

This journal is a gift of "me-time" for you. Let me take you through what to expect as you begin this journey, guided by personal experiences and practical insights. Journalling is more than just writing; it's an intentional act of self-care. Here's how I prepare myself before I begin and you can too.

- **Find your calm space:** I remember the first time I decided to journal it was during my child's nap time. I sat beside her letting the quietness set the mood. Your space doesn't need to be perfect; it just needs to feel like yours.

- **Breathe and set an intention:** Before picking up the pen, I take three deep breaths and ask myself: What do I need today? Some days, it's clarity. On other days, it's simply an outlet for my emotions.

- **Let go of expectations:** When I first started, I worried about writing the "right" thing. Over time, I learned that there's no right or wrong in journalling, it's just you and your thoughts needing an outlet.

What to expect during journalling

Journaling is like peeling layers off an onion it's raw, sometimes messy, but deeply rewarding.

- Clarity: As you write, your thoughts may organise themselves without you even realising it.
- Emotional release: Some days, I have found myself tearing up as I put feelings into words. On other days, I have just used writing to declutter my thoughts.
- Self-discovery: Writing regularly has shown me patterns-things I love, things that drain me, and things I want to change.
- Nothingness: Some days you will open the journal and not feel like writing anything, those days just take time to sit and breathe without forcing yourself to write.

After journalling - the process of embracing the calm

Once you begin to pour your thoughts onto paper, take a moment to reflect. Here's what I do after journaling:

- Pause and reread: I glance back at what I wrote, not to critique but to acknowledge myself. Sometimes, I highlight a phrase that feels powerful.
- Set an intention: I choose a small action for the day. For example: "Today, I will sit in the garden with my child for 10 minutes and enjoy the sun."
- Close with gratitude: I write one thing I'm grateful for. Some words of appreciation or just the courage to show up for myself.
- I keep it close as a reminder that I acknowledge and embrace my imperfect days and keep going on.

How journalling helped me

When I first started, I thought journalling would be just an occasional task for me. But over time, it became a lifeline, my coping skill and a space where I could be myself without judgment. Through regular journalling:

- I began understanding my triggers and joys better.
- The simple act of writing helped me process emotions instead of bottling them up.
- My journals became my emotional outlet and made me feel lighter after releasing my feelings on the paper.
- It helped me feel less cluttered in my mind and more organised on paper, making me feel relaxed.
- It helped me compartmentalise different situations and not mix them all, which gave me clarity in thought.
- Journalling reminded me that self-care isn't selfish, it is an act of self-preservation.

Weekly Planner

Monday

- ◯ __________
- ◯ __________
- ◯ __________
- ◯ __________
- ◯ __________
- ◯ __________
- ◯ __________
- ◯ __________

Tuesday

- ◯ __________
- ◯ __________
- ◯ __________
- ◯ __________
- ◯ __________
- ◯ __________
- ◯ __________
- ◯ __________

Wednesday

- ◯ __________
- ◯ __________
- ◯ __________
- ◯ __________
- ◯ __________
- ◯ __________
- ◯ __________
- ◯ __________

Thursday

- ◯ __________
- ◯ __________
- ◯ __________
- ◯ __________
- ◯ __________
- ◯ __________
- ◯ __________
- ◯ __________

Friday

- ◯ __________
- ◯ __________
- ◯ __________
- ◯ __________
- ◯ __________
- ◯ __________
- ◯ __________
- ◯ __________

Weekend

- ◯ __________
- ◯ __________
- ◯ __________
- ◯ __________
- ◯ __________
- ◯ __________
- ◯ __________
- ◯ __________

SELF-CARE
checklist

BODY

- ☐ SLEEP AT LEAST 8 HOURS
- ☐ MORNING STRETCH
- ☐ 30 MIN WALK OUTSIDE
- ☐ DRINK ENOUGH WATER
- ☐ EAT PROTEIN BREAKFAST
- ☐ MINDFUL EATING
- ☐ SKINCARE ROUTINE
- ☐ COLD SHOWER
- ☐ USE MOISTURISER
- ☐ DECLUTTER AS YOU GO
- ☐ PICK AN OUTFIT YOU LOVE
- ☐ MINDFUL BREATHING

MIND

- ☐ LIMITED SCREEN TIME
- ☐ PICK UP A BOOK TO READ
- ☐ SOCIAL MEDIA DETOX
- ☐ FIND A NEW HOBBY
- ☐ LISTEN TO A PODCAST
- ☐ JOURNAL EVERY DAY
- ☐ LEARN SOMETHING NEW
- ☐ CONNECT WITH LOVED ONES
- ☐ CREATE A VISION BOARD
- ☐ HAVE SOME ALONE TIME

SPIRIT

- ☐ PRACTISE MEDITATION
- ☐ EXPRESS GRATEFULNESS
- ☐ ACKNOWLEDGE EMOTIONS
- ☐ ACTS OF KINDNESS
- ☐ DAILY AFFIRMATIONS
- ☐ PRACTISE MINDFULNESS
- ☐ COMMUNITY WORK
- ☐ POSITIVE THINKING

Setting intention

As a single mother, entrepreneur, and someone who's experienced both personal and professional struggles, I've learned that life doesn't always go according to plan. There were days when I felt completely overwhelmed while juggling a career, solo motherhood, figuring out my life, sorting finances and the emotional aftermath of a difficult divorce.

I remember moments when the to-do lists seemed endless, and my mental health was hanging by a thread. It was during these times that I realised the importance of setting clear intentions not just for my day, but for my life.

I began by setting simple intentions, paying attention to my surroundings, buying myself flowers, taking a pause to admire nature and carving out 15 minutes for myself before the chaos of the day began. These small, intentional practices of self-care helped me big time. As I worked on my own healing and growth.

I started realising that intention-setting isn't just about making big, life-changing resolutions; it's about creating small, meaningful shifts in your daily habits that can transform your mindset.

One of my favourite things to do now is to set an intention each week. For instance, when I first started Sanity Daily, I set the intention to remain grounded, despite single-handedly managing my blog and raising my daughter not to mention working a full-time job to meet ends. I decided that no matter how busy life got, I would create space for growth, learning, and, most importantly, self-compassion.

I still set weekly intentions, sometimes they're about focusing on a new project, and other times they're about giving myself permission to rest. This journal is born from my own experiences setting intentions, working through the struggles, and celebrating the small wins along the way.

Your first task

Take a moment to reflect on what you hope to gain from this process. What is your intention for using this journal? How do you envision it supporting your well-being and personal growth?

 This week, I intend to use this journal as a tool to process my emotions, to create space for self-compassion, and to reflect on my small wins every day.

Feel free to use the following prompts and use the empty space to pour down your thoughts :

- What do I hope to gain from using this journal?
- How can I use this journal to support my emotional well-being and growth?
- What is one intention I can set today to ensure I stay committed to this practice and make space for myself?

P.S. Make it all about you!

Creating your own space

Now that you've set your intention for this journal practice, let's dive into goal-setting. But here's the thing - I'm not talking about a five-year plan or lofty dreams that feel out of reach right now.

We're talking about small, achievable wins that will give you that daily sense of accomplishment and help you feel empowered. You don't need to have everything figured out all at once. Small steps create momentum, and that's where real change begins. I know from my own experience, that when life feels overwhelming, it's easy to get lost in the big picture. That's why I started setting small, intentional goals for myself knowing my capacity. I work a lot and am very passionate about learning new things and doing things in a better way but I constantly remind myself to take a pause and break down things it helps so much when I focus on tiny actions —like spending 10 minutes each day to organise my workspace or to write my to-do list of the day.

Goal - Create your peace corner

To get you started, I am giving you a small goal today - spend 10 minutes to find your peace corner. It could be a corner in your home, a place you like or even a park or cafe. If it is your home, you can begin by decluttering and decorating one area with all your favourite things, all things that bring you joy and calm.

Paste pictures of all your favourite things here or draw them, again make it all about you. Once you are done doing this activity and I hope you enjoy doing this task, you can move to the next set of exercises and take a deep dive into setting some personal goals based on the stage of life you are at.

Go easy and slow!

Sharing a picture of one of my peace corners during COVID times. These tiny steps helped me create a space for my passion, my dedicated area for writing, gave me a sense of control, and motivation to write and most importantly, reminded me that I didn't have to do it all at once.

Some goal-setting exercises for you -
- What is one small goal I can set for myself this week that will make a big difference in my peace of mind?
- How can I break down this goal into manageable, bite-sized steps?

Make Today Better

Anything is Possible

JUST Believe IN yourself

keep trying

Be proud of yourself

Weekly Planner

Monday	**Tuesday**	**Wednesday**
○ ___________	○ ___________	○ ___________
○ ___________	○ ___________	○ ___________
○ ___________	○ ___________	○ ___________
○ ___________	○ ___________	○ ___________
○ ___________	○ ___________	○ ___________
○ ___________	○ ___________	○ ___________
○ ___________	○ ___________	○ ___________
○ ___________	○ ___________	○ ___________
Thursday	**Friday**	**Weekend**
○ ___________	○ ___________	○ ___________
○ ___________	○ ___________	○ ___________
○ ___________	○ ___________	○ ___________
○ ___________	○ ___________	○ ___________
○ ___________	○ ___________	○ ___________
○ ___________	○ ___________	○ ___________
○ ___________	○ ___________	○ ___________
○ ___________	○ ___________	○ ___________

Stress Dump Page

Stress often builds up because we don't give ourselves the space to express what's truly bothering us. The Stress Dump Page is your personal judgment-free space where you can pour out your worries, anger, frustrations, and anxieties onto paper. You will find a few stress dump pages in this journal, use them freely.

By transferring your thoughts from your mind to the page, you lighten the load on your mental space, making room for clarity and calm.

Exercise:

- Spend 10 minutes writing down everything that's on your mind. Don't worry about grammar, spelling, or structure, just let your thoughts flow freely.
- Once done, take a deep breath and reread what you've written. Highlight one or two things that feel most pressing or actionable.
- Ask yourself: What can I control about this? What can I let go of?

Notes from my personal journal

Some days, the weight of the world feels heavy. But today, I want to remember that my strength comes from within. It's not about always being perfect or having it all together, it's about getting back up when I fall. I have weathered storms, and I will weather more. The fire inside me is far stronger than any fear or doubt to take space. Today, I choose to trust myself, even in moments of uncertainty.

Self-Affirmations

Now that you've set your goals - remember this: you've already made progress. No matter how small the steps may feel right now, each one is an achievement. It's easy to get caught up in what we haven't done, but I encourage you to pause for a moment and celebrate what you have done.

Affirmations are a set of positive and powerful words to reinforce self-love and alignment. They work by reprogramming your mindset and reminding you of your strengths. They help shift your focus from self-doubt to self-compassion, from negative self-talk to positive self-talk. And for us mothers, when we are often our own toughest critics, it's time to start treating ourselves with the same compassion we offer to others.

I created this journal because I know how easy it is to forget our worth when life gets overwhelming and never give ourselves enough credit for how far we come along. But as you move through this path with me, I want you to remember that you are worthy of love, rest, and joy.

Five affirmations for you

I am doing my best,
and that is enough.

I am worthy of rest,
and taking time for myself
is a form of self-care.

I am resilient,
and capable of handling
whatever comes my way.

I celebrate the small
wins and honour my
progress every day.

I am kind to myself and
embrace the balance
between giving and
receiving love

The Exercise

Affirmations work by reprogramming your subconscious mind, helping you to replace negative or limiting beliefs with empowering ones. Think of a positive affirmation, write it down 5 times and speak out loud while you write it. Let it sink in, let your soul absorb it.

Use this affirmation daily throughout the week, and watch as it gradually transforms your inner dialogue and strengthens your connection to your true self.

SELF-CARE
checklist

BODY

- ☐ SLEEP AT LEAST 8 HOURS
- ☐ MORNING STRETCH
- ☐ 30 MIN WALK OUTSIDE
- ☐ DRINK ENOUGH WATER
- ☐ EAT PROTEIN BREAKFAST
- ☐ MINDFUL EATING

- ☐ SKINCARE ROUTINE
- ☐ COLD SHOWER
- ☐ USE MOISTURISER
- ☐ DECLUTTER AS YOU GO
- ☐ PICK AN OUTFIT YOU LOVE
- ☐ MINDFUL BREATHING

MIND

- ☐ LIMITED SCREEN TIME
- ☐ PICK UP A BOOK TO READ
- ☐ SOCIAL MEDIA DETOX
- ☐ FIND A NEW HOBBY
- ☐ LISTEN TO A PODCAST

- ☐ JOURNAL EVERY DAY
- ☐ LEARN SOMETHING NEW
- ☐ CONNECT WITH LOVED ONES
- ☐ CREATE A VISION BOARD
- ☐ HAVE SOME ALONE TIME

SPIRIT

- ☐ PRACTISE MEDITATION
- ☐ EXPRESS GRATEFULNESS
- ☐ ACKNOWLEDGE EMOTIONS
- ☐ ACTS OF KINDNESS

- ☐ DAILY AFFIRMATIONS
- ☐ PRACTISE MINDFULNESS
- ☐ COMMUNITY WORK
- ☐ POSITIVE THINKING

Guided Prompt

- One

Write for self-engagement

This journal contains four personalised prompts for mothers to self-engage and feel a sense of calm. These guided prompts or topic suggestions are designed to help you delve into your inner self, recognising the moments that bring you closer to your true essence. By identifying these connections, you strengthen your understanding of yourself and your path in life. the true purpose of this journal and these exercises is to bring your awareness to your inner world and take control of it to live a happier and healthier life.

This week, we are focusing on connecting with our true selves - understanding our desires, acknowledging our emotions, and recognising the values that guide our decisions. Through this task, you will explore these aspects with honesty and depth.

Use the question in the following page as a tool to deepen your self-connection, and revisit it throughout the week if you feel inspired. Be honest, be open, write freely, and let the thoughts flow. Use the next few pages to write your thoughts and feelings.

Now if you are ready, I would want you to take a deep breath and close your eyes for a moment. What does your body need right now -rest, movement, stillness, or connection? How can you honour this need with love and gentleness, even if it's just for a few minutes?

This exercise will encourage you to take a moment for self-care and reflect on how you can prioritise your well-being.

Mindfulness Practice Page

Mindfulness is about grounding yourself in the present moment, offering relief from the constant mental chatter and the rush of daily life. For busy moms, practising mindfulness can be a game-changer, helping to reduce stress, improve focus, and bring a sense of calm. This page guides you through a simple mindfulness exercise that can be done in just 5 minutes because even a few moments of stillness can create a ripple effect of peace throughout your day.

Be honest, be open, follow the 5-minute grounding technique exercise, write freely, and let your thoughts flow. Use the next page to write how are you feeling before the 5-minute grounding technique shared here and the next few pages to write your thoughts and feelings after you practise the technique.

Exercise: 5-Minute Grounding Technique

- Find a quiet space: Sit comfortably and close your eyes.

- Focus on your breath: Breathe deeply through your nose for 4 counts, hold for 4 counts, and exhale through your mouth for 6 counts. Repeat for 5 cycles.

- Engage your senses: Open your eyes and name:
    - 5 things you can see
    - 4 things you can feel
    - 3 things you can hear
    - 2 things you can smell
    - 1 thing you can taste

- Reflect: How does your body feel now compared to before and write it down.

My dearest,

____

You are _______________________________

____

Thank you for _______________________________

____

I love you _______________________________

____

Weekly Planner

Monday

Tuesday

Wednesday

Thursday

Friday

Weekend

Notes from my personal journal

I push myself to the limit, thinking I need to keep going, always striving. But today, I reminded myself that rest is not a weakness, it's a form of self-care. Taking time to recharge allows me to be the best version of myself, and that's important for my relationships with my loved ones.

Act
with
Intention

I can do
Anything

Dream

Stronger
THAN
Yesterday

Embrace
YOUR
Peace

Stress Dump Page

Stress often builds up because we don't give ourselves the space to express what's truly bothering us. The Stress Dump Page is your personal judgment-free space where you can pour out your worries, anger, frustrations, and anxieties onto paper. You will find a few stress dump pages in this journal, use them freely.

By transferring your thoughts from your mind to the page, you lighten the load on your mental space, making room for clarity and calm.

Exercise:

- Spend 10 minutes writing down everything that's on your mind. Don't worry about grammar, spelling, or structure, just let your thoughts flow freely.
- Once done, take a deep breath and reread what you've written. Highlight one or two things that feel most pressing or actionable.
- Ask yourself: What can I control about this? What can I let go of?

SELF-CARE
checklist

☐ SLEEP AT LEAST 8 HOURS

☐ MORNING STRETCH

☐ 30 MIN WALK OUTSIDE

☐ DRINK ENOUGH WATER

☐ EAT PROTEIN BREAKFAST

☐ MINDFUL EATING

☐ SKINCARE ROUTINE

☐ COLD SHOWER

☐ USE MOISTURISER

☐ DECLUTTER AS YOU GO

☐ PICK AN OUTFIT YOU LOVE

☐ MINDFUL BREATHING

☐ LIMITED SCREEN TIME

☐ PICK UP A BOOK TO READ

☐ SOCIAL MEDIA DETOX

☐ FIND A NEW HOBBY

☐ LISTEN TO A PODCAST

☐ JOURNAL EVERY DAY

☐ LEARN SOMETHING NEW

☐ CONNECT WITH LOVED ONES

☐ CREATE A VISION BOARD

☐ HAVE SOME ALONE TIME

☐ PRACTISE MEDITATION

☐ EXPRESS GRATEFULNESS

☐ ACKNOWLEDGE EMOTIONS

☐ ACTS OF KINDNESS

☐ DAILY AFFIRMATIONS

☐ PRACTISE MINDFULNESS

☐ COMMUNITY WORK

☐ POSITIVE THINKING

Guided Prompt

-two

Write to Identify Stressors

As mothers, when we juggle multiple roles, each demanding our attention and energy. It's easy to get caught up in the rush of daily life, but it's essential to take a step back and check in with ourselves. Identifying what's bothering us is a crucial step in taking care of our mental health. When we are aware of the specific situations, people, or responsibilities that cause us stress, we can begin to take control of how we respond to them.

This section invites you to reflect on what has been weighing on your mind lately. Are there recurring stressors that you've been ignoring or brushing aside? By acknowledging them, you give yourself the power to process and address these emotions. It's important to remember that stress doesn't have to be faced alone, reaching out for support from loved ones or professionals can make a world of difference. Think of it as taking small, manageable steps. As you continue to write breaking down your stressors helps you feel less overwhelmed and more empowered.

Just when you are ready, I would want you to think about what has been weighing on my mind lately. Are there specific situations or people that seem to cause you stress? What do you feel can help you to address or release these stressors?

This exercise will help you become aware of the sources of stress in your life, allowing you to process and identify where you might focus your energy in managing or releasing that stress.

Take a moment to breathe
and look back: acknowledge
how far you have come.

Progress Tracker

Tracking your progress isn't just about accountability, it is about celebrating your efforts, no matter how small. This page lets you reflect on how consistently you've shown up for yourself during the week. It's not about perfection but about progress, reminding you that every small step you take matters in your journey toward balance and well-being.

Use the simple tracker shared on the next page to reflect on your journey with the journal and how it is making you feel.

Reflect on Your Growth:
Write a short note about how engaging in these practices made you feel before and after. Did you notice shifts in your mood or energy?

Share Your Journey:
If you're comfortable, share your progress by posting pictures or notes on social media and tagging @TheTherapeuticJournal. Celebrate your wins and inspire other moms on the same path!

Track Your Progress

This exercise helps you monitor your emotional, mental, and self-care progress as you journal.

Begin by reflecting on where you are right now. Use the following prompts to record your current state:

- Emotionally: How do you feel most days? (e.g., overwhelmed, calm, stressed, content)
- Mentally: How clear and focused is your mind? (e.g., scattered, peaceful, overburdened)
- Self-Care: How much time are you currently dedicating to yourself? (e.g., none, some, consistent)
- Other Areas: Add specific areas you want to track (e.g., physical health, parenting moments, relationship quality).

Today, I feel:

Emotionally:_______________________________

Mentally:_________________________________

Self-Care:________________________________

Other: __________________________________

Notes from my personal journal

I am not my mistakes, my past, or anyone's opinion of me. I am my dreams, my resilience, my persistence and the fire that keeps burning inside me. Today, I choose to walk with pride with my head high because I am doing my best and showing up for myself, always have been, and always will be.

Guided Prompt

-three

Write to Vent Out

We often carry the weight of many emotions - stress, frustration, exhaustion, and sometimes even guilt. Bottling these feelings up can be incredibly draining and, over time, it can affect our mental health. Venting out is a powerful way to release pent-up emotions and regain a sense of emotional balance.

This prompt encourages you to let it all out, without judgment or fear. By putting your feelings into words, you're giving yourself permission to own your emotions. It's okay to feel upset, angry, or overwhelmed what matters is that you acknowledge these feelings and give yourself space to process them. When we suppress our emotions, they can fester and create unnecessary tension. But when we express them, we create room for healing.

Writing down your frustrations or stressors can bring clarity, help you better understand what's triggering your emotions, and even help you identify patterns in your behaviour or responses.Venting out isn't about complaining it's about honouring your emotions and giving yourself the freedom to feel, so you can move forward with greater peace.

Write down everything that's frustrating or overwhelming you right now. Let it all out without judgment or fear. How do I feel after expressing these emotions?

This venting-out prompt is your safe space to release pent-up emotions and frustrations, offering a therapeutic outlet for processing overwhelming feelings.

The Self-Love Letter

Today I will encourage you to write a letter to yourself. Not to your younger self or your older self. Just some words you want to hear, some kind words you want someone to say to you, say it to yourself.

Purpose: To nurture yourself with kind, affirming words, especially on days when you might feel overwhelmed.

1. Imagine you are writing a letter to yourself but from a place of deep love and care. Think of it as a message of encouragement from a loving friend or a parent.
2. Start with: Dear [Your Name], I see you. I see how hard you work. I see how much love you give every day.
3. Write about everything you appreciate about yourself as a mother, a woman, and as an individual.
4. Conclude the letter with words of compassion, reminding yourself that you deserve love and rest and that you are doing your best.
5. Read it on days when you need to remind yourself of your worth.

Guided Prompt
-four

Write to Gain Clarity

As mothers, our minds are often filled with endless to-do lists, worries, and emotions. It's easy to feel overwhelmed by the sheer volume of thoughts swirling around. But gaining clarity starts with articulating those feelings and putting them into words. When we take the time to reflect on what's going on inside, we can begin to untangle the chaos and find peace in the process.

This section invites you to express what's on your mind, to make sense of your emotions, and to break down what's been clouding your mental space. When you put pen to paper, you create order from the noise. Writing can help you gain a fresh perspective on your struggles, uncover underlying causes of stress, and even identify the simple steps you can take to feel more centred.

By articulating your emotions, you free yourself from the burden of carrying them in silence. It's not about finding all the answers right away, it's about creating the space to reflect, understand, and release what no longer serves you.

Sit in a comfortable position and see your life as a third person. Try to step back and look at your life from a distance, try to notice what is the one thing that would bring you the most peace or relief. How can you begin to take steps toward it, no matter how small?

This clarity-seeking exercise encourages reflection on what truly matters to you and provides a path for actionable steps to create more peace in your life.

Weekly Planner

Monday	**Tuesday**	**Wednesday**
○ _______	○ _______	○ _______
○ _______	○ _______	○ _______
○ _______	○ _______	○ _______
○ _______	○ _______	○ _______
○ _______	○ _______	○ _______
○ _______	○ _______	○ _______
○ _______	○ _______	○ _______
○ _______	○ _______	○ _______
Thursday	**Friday**	**Weekend**
○ _______	○ _______	○ _______
○ _______	○ _______	○ _______
○ _______	○ _______	○ _______
○ _______	○ _______	○ _______
○ _______	○ _______	○ _______
○ _______	○ _______	○ _______
○ _______	○ _______	○ _______
○ _______	○ _______	○ _______

Gratitude Reflection — *thankful*

Gratitude is a powerful tool for shifting your mindset. Even on the hardest days, finding moments of joy or kindness can help you focus on the positive and cultivate resilience. Practising gratitude helps you to embrace the good, the bad and everything in between. These pages are your moments to pause, reflect, and acknowledge the good things in your life big or small.

Practicing gratitude regularly can improve your mood, increase your sense of well-being, and remind you of how far you have come.

Exercise:

- Write about three moments you're thankful for this week. They can be as simple as a kind word from a stranger, a hug from your child, or the peacefulness of a quiet morning coffee.
- Reflect on why these moments matter to you. How did they make you feel? What did they teach you?

Releasing Negative Thoughts

This exercise will help you release negative emotions and make space for calm and positivity.

- Take a deep breath, and close your eyes for a moment.
- Write down a negative thought or emotion you've been carrying (e.g., stress, guilt, anger).
- Reflect on this thought - where is it coming from? What do you need to release it?
- Now, write down a positive counter-thought or affirmation that can replace it (e.g., "I am doing the best I can, and that's enough.")
- Let go of the negative thought by symbolically crossing it out, erasing it, or writing it on a piece of scrap paper to tear up or throw away.
- Conclude with a moment of deep breathing, allowing the positive affirmation to settle in.

Stress Dump Page

Stress often builds up because we don't give ourselves the space to express what's truly bothering us. The Stress Dump Page is your personal judgment-free space where you can pour out your worries, anger, frustrations, and anxieties onto paper. You will find a few stress dump pages in this journal, use them freely.

By transferring your thoughts from your mind to the page, you lighten the load on your mental space, making room for clarity and calm.

Exercise:

- Spend 10 minutes writing down everything that's on your mind. Don't worry about grammar, spelling, or structure, just let your thoughts flow freely.
- Once done, take a deep breath and reread what you've written. Highlight one or two things that feel most pressing or actionable.
- Ask yourself: What can I control about this? What can I let go of?

My dearest,

You are

Thank you for

I love you

Notes from my personal journal

The most important relationship I'll ever have is the one I nurture with myself. I'm learning to show up for myself even on the hard days. I'm learning to be my own safe place and that's the greatest act of love I can give.

The Mindful Pause

This simple exercise will help you to slow down your thoughts and become more present in your day.

- Set a timer for 3-5 minutes.
- Find a comfortable seated position, ensuring that your feet are grounded and your spine is straight.
- Close your eyes and begin taking slow, deliberate breaths. Inhale deeply through your nose, hold for a moment, and then exhale slowly through your mouth.
- With each breath, allow your body to relax deeper. Notice any areas of tension whether it's your shoulders, jaw, or hands and gently let them soften with each breath.
- As thoughts come to mind, acknowledge them without judgment and gently return your focus to your breathing. It's okay if your mind wanders simply bring it back to the present moment.
- When the timer goes off, take one last deep breath and open your eyes gently.

SELF-CARE
checklist

BODY

- ☐ SLEEP AT LEAST 8 HOURS
- ☐ MORNING STRETCH
- ☐ 30 MIN WALK OUTSIDE
- ☐ DRINK ENOUGH WATER
- ☐ EAT PROTEIN BREAKFAST
- ☐ MINDFUL EATING
- ☐ SKINCARE ROUTINE
- ☐ COLD SHOWER
- ☐ USE MOISTURISER
- ☐ DECLUTTER AS YOU GO
- ☐ PICK AN OUTFIT YOU LOVE
- ☐ MINDFUL BREATHING

MIND

- ☐ LIMITED SCREEN TIME
- ☐ PICK UP A BOOK TO READ
- ☐ SOCIAL MEDIA DETOX
- ☐ FIND A NEW HOBBY
- ☐ LISTEN TO A PODCAST
- ☐ JOURNAL EVERY DAY
- ☐ LEARN SOMETHING NEW
- ☐ CONNECT WITH LOVED ONES
- ☐ CREATE A VISION BOARD
- ☐ HAVE SOME ALONE TIME

SPIRIT

- ☐ PRACTISE MEDITATION
- ☐ EXPRESS GRATEFULNESS
- ☐ ACKNOWLEDGE EMOTIONS
- ☐ ACTS OF KINDNESS
- ☐ DAILY AFFIRMATIONS
- ☐ PRACTISE MINDFULNESS
- ☐ COMMUNITY WORK
- ☐ POSITIVE THINKING

Free writing Space

Free writing is a valuable practice for deepening self-awareness and personal growth. It offers a way to connect with your innermost thoughts and emotions without the constraints of formal exercises.

Feel free to use this unstructured blank space to support emotional processing and creativity, making it a crucial component of a holistic journalling practice.

Track Your Progress

This exercise helps you monitor your emotional, mental, and self-care progress as you journal.

Begin by reflecting on where you are right now. Use the following prompts to record your current state:

- Emotionally: How do you feel most days? (e.g., overwhelmed, calm, stressed, content)
- Mentally: How clear and focused is your mind? (e.g., scattered, peaceful, overburdened)
- Self-Care: How much time are you currently dedicating to yourself? (e.g., none, some, consistent)
- Other Areas: Add specific areas you want to track (e.g., physical health, parenting moments, relationship quality).

Today, I feel:
Emotionally:_______________________________
Mentally:_______________________________
Self-Care:_______________________________
Other: _______________________________

Notes from my personal journal

I used to think shedding old parts of myself was a loss. Now, I see it as growth. The girl I was taught me to love and the woman I am teaches me to let go with grace. Both versions of me are equally imperative and make me whole and complete.

FOR SPECIAL
notes

2025

JANUARY

Su	Mo	Tu	We	Th	Fr	Sa
			1	2	3	4
5	6	7	8	9	10	11
12	13	14	15	16	17	18
19	20	21	22	23	24	25
26	27	28	29	30	31	

FEBRUARY

Su	Mo	Tu	We	Th	Fr	Sa
						1
2	3	4	5	6	7	8
9	10	11	12	13	14	15
16	17	18	19	20	21	22
23	24	25	26	27	28	

MARCH

Su	Mo	Tu	We	Th	Fr	Sa
						1
2	3	4	5	6	7	8
9	10	11	12	13	14	15
16	17	18	19	20	21	22
23	24	25	26	27	28	29
30	31					

APRIL

Su	Mo	Tu	We	Th	Fr	Sa
		1	2	3	4	5
6	7	8	9	10	11	12
13	14	15	16	17	18	19
20	21	22	23	24	25	26
27	28	29	30			

MAY

Su	Mo	Tu	We	Th	Fr	Sa
				1	2	3
4	5	6	7	8	9	10
11	12	13	14	15	16	17
18	19	20	21	22	23	24
25	26	27	28	29	30	31

JUNE

Su	Mo	Tu	We	Th	Fr	Sa
1	2	3	4	5	6	7
8	9	10	11	12	13	14
15	16	17	18	19	20	21
22	23	24	25	26	27	28
29	30					

JULY

Su	Mo	Tu	We	Th	Fr	Sa
		1	2	3	4	5
6	7	8	9	10	11	12
13	14	15	16	17	18	19
20	21	22	23	24	25	26
27	28	29	30	31		

AUGUST

Su	Mo	Tu	We	Th	Fr	Sa
					1	2
3	4	5	6	7	8	9
10	11	12	13	14	15	16
17	18	19	20	21	22	23
24	25	26	27	28	29	30
31						

SEPTEMBER

Su	Mo	Tu	We	Th	Fr	Sa
	1	2	3	4	5	6
7	8	9	10	11	12	13
14	15	16	17	18	19	20
21	22	23	24	25	26	27
28	29	30				

OCTOBER

Su	Mo	Tu	We	Th	Fr	Sa
			1	2	3	4
5	6	7	8	9	10	11
12	13	14	15	16	17	18
19	20	21	22	23	24	25
26	27	28	29	30	31	

NOVEMBER

Su	Mo	Tu	We	Th	Fr	Sa
						1
2	3	4	5	6	7	8
9	10	11	12	13	14	15
16	17	18	19	20	21	22
23	24	25	26	27	28	29
30						

DECEMBER

Su	Mo	Tu	We	Th	Fr	Sa
	1	2	3	4	5	6
7	8	9	10	11	12	13
14	15	16	17	18	19	20
21	22	23	24	25	26	27
28	29	30	31			

Dear Reader,

I want to thank you for trusting this journal to be a part of your journey. Every word you have written, every moment you have spent reflecting, and every small step you have taken toward self-care is proof of your strength and commitment to yourself.

This journal is not just pages bound together; it is a witness to your growth, your resilience, and your incredible ability to overcome life challenges with grace. It will stay with you forever. I am proud of you for showing up for yourself.

This journal may come to an end, but your journey doesn't. Now you are better equipped with the tools, insights, and mindset to continue prioritising yourself. Life will have its challenges, but you now have a space within yourself to come back to - a space of calm, strength, and hope.

I'd love to hear about your experience with this journal. Share your thoughts, your favourite exercises, or a special moment it helped you through.

If you feel comfortable, tag @TheTherapeuticJournal on Instagram to inspire other moms to start their journey, or you can email us at writeus@therapeutic-journal.com

Stay connected at -www.therapeutic-journal.com

Keep moving forward, one step at a time.
You got this!